PUMPKIN CARVING STENCILS

> FOR ADVANCED <

Copyrights © Gobble Jackblood

MW01173181

HOW TO USE THE CARVING STENCILS?

MOST OF THE STENCILS IN THIS BOOK ARE FOR ADVANCED CARVERS. THE BLACK PART OF THE PATTERN IS THE PART TO BE CUT OUT OF THE PUMPKIN. START CARVING FROM THE CENTRE OF THE PATTERN AND HEAD OUTWARDS.

LATER IN THE BOOK, I HAVE OUTLINED TWO WAYS TO CARVE PATTERNS IN A PUMPKIN.

METHOD 1:

1. FIRST CLEAN THE PUMPKIN BY SCRAPING THE FLESH IN THE AREA WHERE YOU WILL CARVE THE PATTERN.

2. CUT OUT A WHOLE PAGE OF YOUR CHOSEN PATTERN FROM THE BOOK USING SCISSORS ALONG THE DOTTED LINES. THEN CUT OFF THE EXCESS PAPER.

3. MAKE SURE THE PUMPKIN IS DRY, THEN STICK THE PATTERN ONTO IT WITH STICKY TAPE. MAKE SURE THE TAPE IS STUCK ON TIGHTLY. USE A PENCIL TO MAKE HOLES CLOSE TOGETHER ALONG THE BLACK OUTLINES, PIERCING THE PAPER.

4. ONCE ALL THE HOLES HAVE BEEN MADE, PEEL OFF THE PAPER AND TAPE TO REVEAL THE PATTERN YOU HAVE JUST MADE. YOU CAN RUB FLOUR INTO THE HOLES IN THE PUMPKIN TO HELP LOCATE THEM. USE THIN CRAFT KNIVES OR WOOD CUTTERS TO CUT OUT THE PATTERN.

5. PLACE THE CANDLE OR BATTERY LAMP INSIDE AND CLOSE THE LID.

METHOD 2:

1. FIRST CLEAN THE PUMPKIN BY SCRAPING THE FLESH IN THE AREA WHERE YOU WILL CARVE THE PATTERN.

2. CUT OUT A WHOLE PAGE OF YOUR CHOSEN PATTERN FROM THE BOOK USING SCISSORS ALONG THE DOTTED LINES. THEN CUT OFF THE EXCESS PAPER.

3. SOAK THE PATTERN IN WATER FOR A FEW SECONDS SO IT WILL STICK BETTER TO THE PUMPKIN. APPLY THE PATTERN TO THE PUMPKIN. THE WET PAPER SHOULD STICK TO IT. TRY TO FIT THE PATTERN TO THE SHAPE OF THE PUMPKIN. THERE MAY BE INFLECTION LINES, BUT DON'T WORRY ABOUT THEM.

4. WRAP THE PATTERN SEVERAL TIMES IN STRETCH FILM TO HOLD THE PUMPKIN BETTER. USE THIN CRAFT KNIVES OR WOOD CUTTERS TO CUT OUT THE PATTERN. WHEN FINISHED, REMOVE THE STRETCH FILM AND PAPER PATTERN, AND WIPE THE PUMPKIN WITH A CLOTH OR PAPER TOWEL.

5. PLACE THE CANDLE OR BATTERY LAMP INSIDE AND CLOSE THE LID.

HAVE FUN!

PAGE 9

PAGE 11

PAGE 13

PAGE 15

PAGE 17

PAGE 19

PAGE 21

PAGE 23

PAGE 25

PAGE 27

PAGE 49

PAGE 51

PAGE 53

PAGE 55

PAGE 57

PAGE 59

PAGE 61

PAGE 63

PAGE 65

PAGE 67

PAGE 69

PAGE 71

PAGE 73

PAGE 75

PAGE 77

PAGE 79

PAGE 81

PAGE 83

PAGE 85

PAGE 87

PAGE 89

PAGE 91

PAGE 93

PAGE 95

PAGE 97

PAGE 99

PAGE 101

PAGE 103

PAGE 105

PAGE 107

Instructions on page 2

Instructions on page 2 11

Instructions on page 2 13

Instructions on page 2

15

Instructions on page 2

17

Instructions on page 2

19

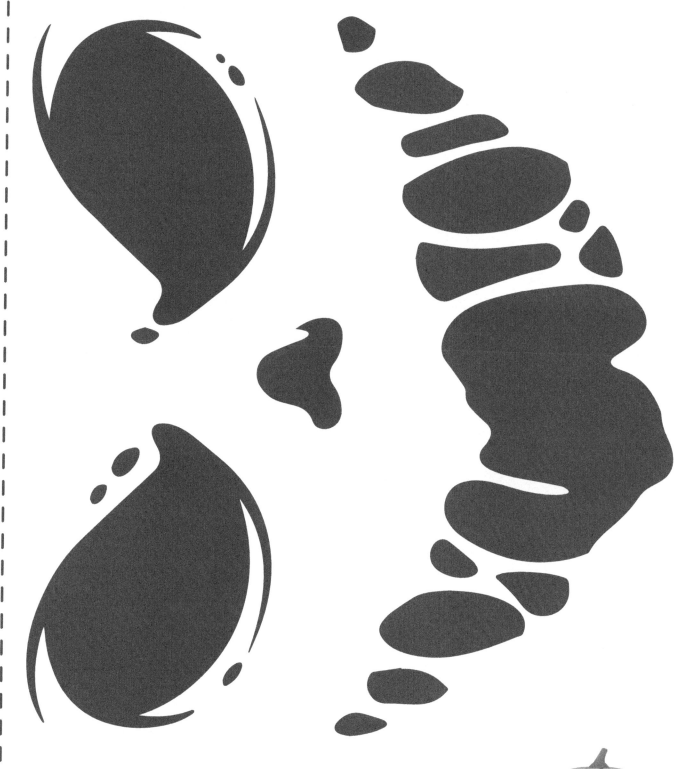

Instructions on page 2

Instructions on page 2

Instructions on page 2

25

Instructions on page 2

Instructions on page 2

Instructions on page 2

31

 **Instructions on page 2**

Instructions on page 2

Instructions on page 2

Instructions on page 2

Instructions on page 2

Instructions on page 1

Instructions on page 2

Instructions on page 2

Instructions on page 2

Instructions on page 2

47

Instructions on page 2

Instructions on page 2

51

TRICK TREAT

TRICK TREAT

Instructions on page 2

Instructions on page 2

Instructions on page 2

Instructions on page 2

Instructions on page 2

Instructions on page 2

Instructions on page 2

Instructions on page 2

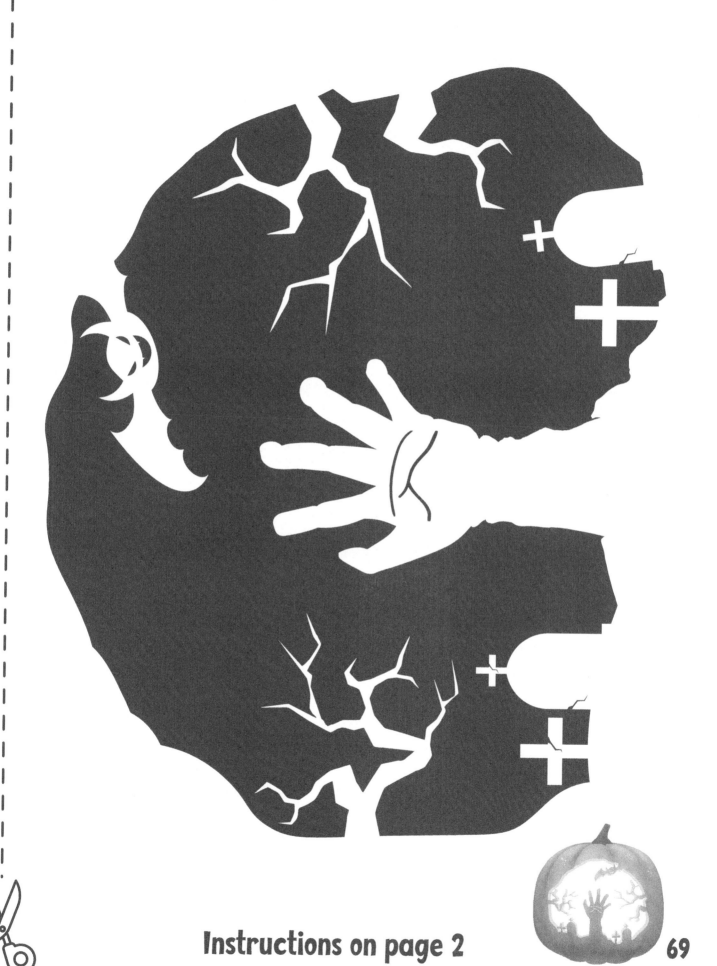

Instructions on page 2

Instructions on page 2

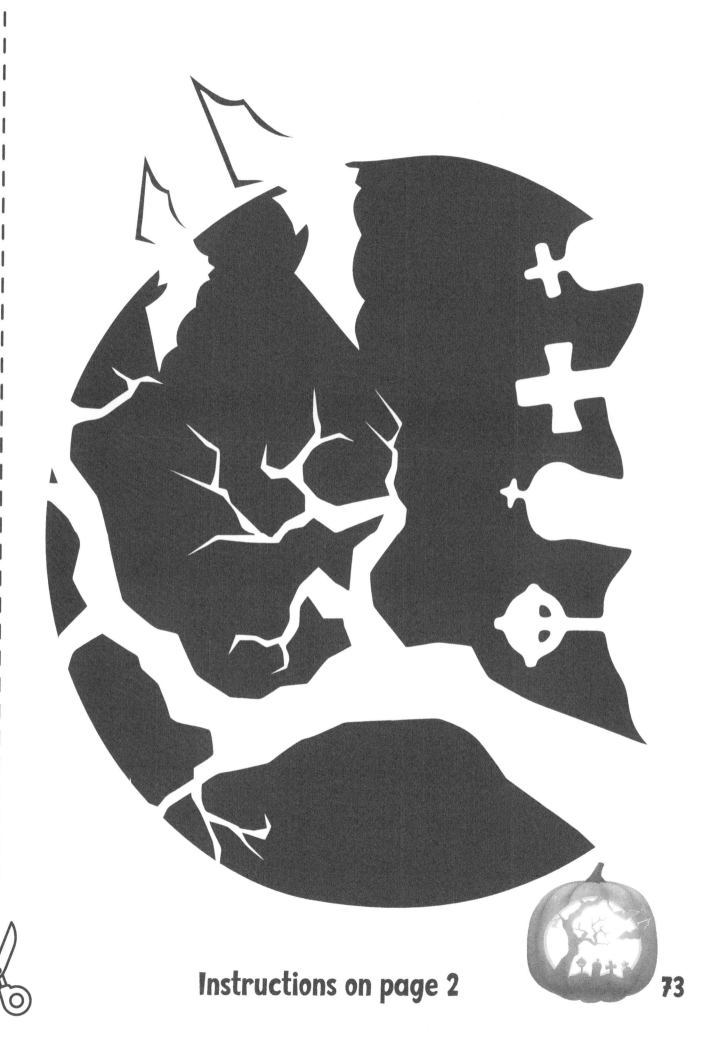

Instructions on page 2

Instructions on page 2

Instructions on page 2

79

Instructions on page 2

Instructions on page 2

Instructions on page 1

Instructions on page 2

Instructions on page 2

89

Instructions on page 2

Instructions on page 2

Instructions on page 2

Instructions on page 2

Instructions on page 2

Instructions on page 2

Instructions on page 2

Instructions on page 2

Instructions on page 2

Made in the USA
Middletown, DE
14 October 2023

40782636R00064